PHJC

P9-AQF-022

COOKING
THE
POLISH
WAY

Lerner Publications Company
A division of Lerner Publishing Group
241 First Avenue North
Minneapolis, MN 55401 U.S.A.

Website address: www.lernerbooks.com

Library of Congress Cataloging-in-Publication Data

Zamojska-Hutchins, Danuta.
    Cooking the Polish way / by Danuta Zamojska-Hutchins.— Rev. & expanded.
        p.   cm. — (Easy menu ethnic cookbooks)
    Includes index.
    Summary: Introduces the land, culture, and cuisine of Poland and includes recipes for soups, salads, main dishes, and side dishes. Includes material on healthy, low-fat, vegetarian cooking, and holidays and festivals.
    ISBN: 0–8225–4119–X (lib. bdg. : alk. paper)
    1. Cookery, Polish—Juvenile literature. 2. Poland—Social life and customs—Juvenile literature. [1. Cookery, Polish. 2. Poland—Social life and customs.] I. Title. II. Series.
    TX723.5.P6 Z3 2002
    641.59438—dc21   2001002962

Manufactured in the United States of America
1 2 3 4 5 6 – AM – 07 06 05 04 03 02

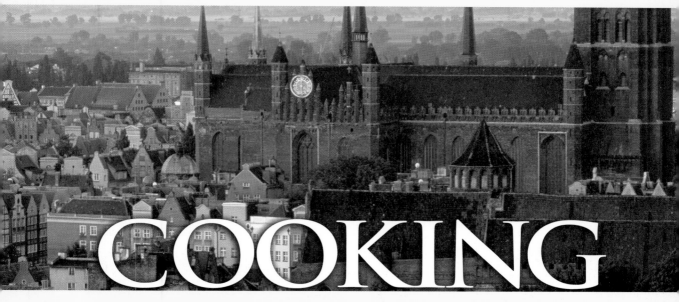

easy menu ethnic cookbooks

COOKING

revised and expanded

THE

to include new low-fat

POLISH

and vegetarian recipes

WAY

Danuta Zamojska-Hutchins

Lerner Publications Company • Minneapolis

Contents

Introduction

Polish people, whether living in Poland or in other parts of the world, have a fierce love for their country. They pride themselves on a strong national identity, something they have had to struggle to keep throughout their nation's thousand-year history—a history that has included numerous invasions and conquests by other countries. Food, though it has often been scarce in Poland, is nevertheless a very important part of Polish heritage and culture. Polish cooking is rich, hearty, and varied in its many flavors and textures. Over hundreds of years, it has been influenced by a strong farming tradition, the available food resources (such as an abundance of fish and grains), and repeated contact with other cultures and cuisines.

Preparing and eating food in Poland marks almost all social occasions, particularly family get-togethers. Such gatherings may celebrate name days (days associated with certain Christian saints) or the church holidays that are a part of Poland's long-standing Roman Catholic tradition, or they may be for no reason other than to share each others' company and conversation over a good meal.

Traditional Polish pierożki, served steaming hot, can be enjoyed as appetizers or as part of the main meal. (Recipe on page 42.)

Baltic Sea

RUSSIA

LITHUANIA

Gdansk

GERMANY

Vistula River

Warsaw

POLAND

BELARUS

Kraków

CARPATHIAN MOUNTAINS

CZECH REPUBLIC

UKRAINE

SLOVAKIA

TATRA MOUNTAINS

The Land

The name Poland comes from the Polish word for "fields" or "plains" (pola), since much of the country is flat. Located in central Europe, Poland is bordered by the Baltic Sea and Russia to the north, Lithuania, Belarus, and Ukraine to the east, the Czech Republic and Slovakia to the south, and Germany to the west.

The Baltic coast of Poland is made up of sandy beaches, sand dunes, and high, forested shores. Poland's major seaport, Gdansk, is located on this coast. Directly south of the Baltic coast is the lakes region, a popular place to vacation because of the many beautiful lakes and forests found there.

The area around Warsaw was first settled about one thousand years ago, and the city became the nation's capital in 1596. Although most of Warsaw was destroyed during World War II (1939–1945), the city was rebuilt and includes beautiful palaces, parks, and public squares. The central plains in the middle of the country make up Poland's largest agricultural area. Warsaw is located on the banks of the Vistula River in this central region. South of Warsaw, the land gradually begins to rise into low mountains and broad valleys. Higher hills dominate the landscape of western and south central Poland, the most densely populated part of the country. In southeastern Poland, rolling hills covered with fruit orchards and forests create beautiful views.

The southernmost part of the country rises steeply into the rugged, wild Tatra Mountains—part of the Carpathian mountain range—where several national parks can be found. The people who live in this remote region follow more of the old folk traditions than most people in modern Poland. They have preserved their regional dialect, dress, and traditional occupation of raising sheep. They are known for their sheep-milk products and hand-spun wool, as well as for their wood sculptures, tapestries, and glass paintings, many of which are exported to the United States.

The Food

The Baltic Sea, along with Poland's many inland lakes and rivers, provides the nation with an abundance of seafood. Carp, flounder, salmon, trout, and herring are all caught by Polish fishing crews and served up in tasty dishes by Polish cooks. Grains such as wheat, rye, and barley are grown on much of the rich farmland in Poland, and Poles enjoy many types of breads and noodles. Crops

Sheep graze in the Polish countryside. Raising sheep is still a common occupation in the rural areas of the country.

such as potatoes, sugar beets, and sunflowers also thrive, and many cooks grow their own supplies of beets, cabbage, and carrots, three important foods in Polish cooking. Although meat is not eaten in abundance in modern Poland, a large number of wild boars once inhabited the country's forests, making pork the most traditional meat served on Polish tables.

Poland was ruled by kings and queens for hundreds of years. Many of these royal figures married foreign princesses and princes, and with each foreign marriage came a new cuisine. A long history of changing borders and rulers has also expanded the national menu. Hungarian goulash, Italian vegetables and pasta, French pastries, and Ukrainian borscht have all found their way into Polish cooking. Over the years, however, the Polish people have adapted these foreign foods to suit their own tastes, and a unique Polish cuisine has been the result.

The People

In addition to their great love of country, the Polish people have a great love of national culture. The arts have an important place in Poland, from traditional folk crafts and dance to painting and classical music. Festivals and fairs celebrating the arts are a common occurrence from bustling Warsaw to remote villages.

Polish people also love to entertain, and they are well known for their hospitality. An old Polish proverb, *Gość w dom, Bóg w dom* ("A guest in the home is God in the home"), is taken very seriously by most Poles. To be a guest in a Polish home is to be treated like royalty, and food is always served. An unannounced guest can expect at least a snack of tea and pastries. Guests who have been invited to a Polish home for dinner will probably sit down to a seven- or eight-course meal!

Although you may not be making many seven-course meals, you should make any recipe in this book with great care. Then, when you serve the food, do as the Poles do and sit down with your family or friends and enjoy every bite of food, as well as some friendly conversation. As the Poles say, *"Smacznego,"* or, "Have a tasty meal!"

Holidays and Festivals

Having a tasty meal is a favorite way of celebrating a Polish holiday. Poland's many Roman Catholics have long observed religious fasts. But fasting and feasting go hand in hand in Poland, for at the end of each fast is a tremendous feast!

Easter, which may fall anytime between late March and late April, is one of the most important religious holidays in Poland. Lent (the forty days prior to Easter) is a solemn time of fasting and prayer for Roman Catholics, and many Polish families eat few meat dishes or sweets during this period. On Good Friday (the Friday before Easter), little or nothing is eaten. The day is spent visiting local churches, each of which presents a display representing Jesus' tomb. Some families may have a very simple dinner of herring, potatoes, or soup before bed.

On the Saturday before Easter, Polish households, decorated with pussy willows and evergreen garlands, bustle with activity. Cooks prepare a tempting variety of dishes for the feast of the following day. The Easter table is set with a white tablecloth and a centerpiece of a springtime lamb (usually made of sugar), a bowl of brightly colored eggs, and a bouquet of fresh hyacinths. Another important part of this day is the blessing of the Easter foods. Families fill a basket with a sampling of their Easter treats, usually including bread, salt, hard-boiled eggs, cold meats, an assortment of desserts, and a small lamb made of butter. These baskets are then taken to church, where a priest blesses their contents. Through this ritual, the special meal of the following day is also blessed.

On Sunday morning, families attend Easter Mass and then hurry home for the wonderful meal. Guests are always welcome, and each person is met by the host to share part of a hard-boiled egg. At last, everyone settles in to enjoy the delicious feast. Typical dishes include soups, baked ham, sausages, roast beef or veal, salads, sauces, and relishes. A selection of delectable desserts, such as the traditional *babkas* and *mazureks*, makes the meal complete.

The day after Easter, a unique Polish tradition is practiced by young people, especially in rural areas and small towns. Also called Dyngus Day, Easter Monday is a time for Polish boys and young men to splash girls and young women with water. These encounters can be as harmless as a sprinkling of a few drops or as drenching as a bucketful of water over the head. Although no one knows for certain the origins of this long-standing tradition, it remains popular in modern times, and Polish girls keep a sharp eye out for lurking boys on Dyngus Day.

Second only to Easter in religious significance, Christmas is a festive time in Poland. Preparations begin a few days before December 25, as families clean their homes, pick out Christmas trees, and buy gifts and food. In large cities and towns, squares and markets bustle with busy vendors and shoppers. On Christmas Eve day, Polish children help trim the family Christmas tree with traditional decorations, including apples, nuts, candy, and homemade ornaments of straw or paper.

Christmas Eve is a day of fasting, which is broken by a dinner called the Wigilia. This special meal is not eaten until a member of the family, usually a child, spots the first evening star in the winter sky. The Christmas Eve table is covered with a snow-white linen

Young men splash these unsuspecting women with water as the traditional Dyngus Day prank.

cloth and set with the family's best dishes. An extra place is always set at the table on this night for any unexpected visitor. Candles are lit, and a small bundle of straw or hay is placed underneath the tablecloth, symbolizing the manger that the baby Jesus slept in. The hay also represents peace, the family's good deeds during Advent (the period beginning four Sundays before Christmas), and their hopes for the future. In the center of the table is the opłatek, the Christmas wafer, which is traditionally baked by nuns and blessed by a priest. Before the meal, the family shares this special wafer while offering good wishes to one another. In some rural areas, part of the wafer is also offered to the family's livestock, in honor of the animals that were present at Jesus' birth.

At last it's time for the carefully prepared dinner. Although meatless, this is a holiday feast that may consist of as many as twelve courses. Typical dishes include beet or mushroom soup, a main course of fish, and a variety of side dishes and desserts. Mushrooms are a popular ingredient, and poppy seeds are in many of the traditional desserts. Every bite is savored and enjoyed by all.

After the big meal, many Polish families enjoy singing their favorite Christmas carols. Another popular pastime is predicting the future by reading the smoke from the candles on the table and by drawing pieces of straw from beneath the tablecloth. Some families open gifts, while others wait until Christmas Day. As it grows later, families get ready to go to their local churches for the Pasterka, or Shepherd's Mass. This service begins at midnight and doesn't end until after 2:00 A.M. on Christmas morning.

Christmas Day is a calm, quiet day for most Polish families. Many people pay visits to friends and relatives, and some enjoy caroling. Guests are always welcome to share a sweet treat and to warm up with a hot beverage such as tea, coffee, or apple cider. The day after Christmas, also known as Saint Stephen's Day, is the last day of vacation for many people and may be spent paying more visits, caroling, and relaxing.

Polish youngsters enjoy cotton candy at a Children's Day festival in Wroclaw, Poland.

On New Year's Eve, many people throw or attend festive parties or fancy dinners and dances. It is an evening to make predictions and wishes for the coming year and to bid farewell to the old. At the stroke of midnight, the new year is welcomed in with great happiness and excitement.

This time of year is also the beginning of the Polish carnival season, and a popular activity is the *kulig*, or sleigh ride. Bundled in their warmest clothes, Polish families and friends pile into horse-drawn sleighs and go from house to house, stopping for food, dancing, and singing before picking up more passengers and traveling on to the neighbors'. Most kuligs also journey into the snowy forests, where riders light a bonfire, heat up a hearty pot of *bigos* (hunter's stew), and celebrate into the night.

In addition to these major holidays, festivals and fairs are held all over Poland throughout the year. Constitution Day in May and

Dancers in traditional Polish costumes celebrate the season at the Harvest Festival.

Independence Day in November commemorate important political events in the nation's history, and Polish children enjoy a special day in their honor in June. One of the oldest customs is the Dozynki (Harvest Festival), which usually takes place in late summer or early autumn, depending on the region and the crop. Farming communities throughout the country celebrate the season's harvest with parades, music, and food. The traditional symbol of the celebration is the *wieniec*, or harvest wreath. These wreaths are woven in different shapes and sizes and are carefully decorated using the fruit of the fields, from grain and flowers to apples and nuts. The wreaths are blessed at local churches before being carried back to family farms in festive processions. A girl or young woman, usually one who has helped with the farmwork and the harvesting, leads the procession, wearing a small wreath on her head. The whole group then enjoys a great feast, along with singing, dancing, and conversation.

No matter what the occasion in Poland, feasting and fun are sure to play an important role. The country's long-standing customs are carried on and enriched in modern times, even as new traditions develop to celebrate Polish culture, history, and cuisine.

Before You Begin

Polish cooking makes use of some ingredients that you may not know. Sometimes special cookware is used, too, although the recipes in this book can easily be prepared with ordinary utensils and pans.

The most important thing you need to know before you start is how to be a careful cook. On the following page, you'll find a few rules that will make your cooking experience safe, fun, and easy. Next, take a look at the "dictionary" of utensils, terms, and special ingredients. You may also want to read the list of tips on preparing healthy, low-fat meals.

When you've picked out a recipe to try, read through it from beginning to end. Now you are ready to shop for ingredients and to organize the cookware you will need. Once you have assembled everything, you're ready to begin cooking.

A bowl of thick and hearty bigos, or hunter's stew, is a great way to warm up on a cold day. (Recipe on page 34.)

The Careful Cook

Whenever you cook, there are certain safety rules you must always keep in mind. Even experienced cooks follow these rules when they are in the kitchen.

- Always wash your hands before handling food. Thoroughly wash all raw vegetables and fruits to remove dirt, chemicals, and insecticides. Wash uncooked poultry, fish, and meat under cold water.
- Use a cutting board when cutting up vegetables and fruits. Don't cut them up in your hand! And be sure to cut in a direction *away* from you and your fingers.
- Long hair or loose clothing can easily catch fire if brought near the burners of a stove. If you have long hair, tie it back before you start cooking.
- Turn all pot handles toward the back of the stove so that you will not catch your sleeves or jewelry on them. This is especially important when younger brothers and sisters are around. They could easily knock off a pot and get burned.
- Always use a pot holder to steady hot pots or to take pans out of the oven. Don't use a wet cloth on a hot pan because the steam it produces could burn you.
- Lift the lid of a steaming pot with the opening away from you so that you will not get burned.
- If you get burned, hold the burn under cold running water. Do not put grease or butter on it. Cold water helps to take the heat out, but grease or butter will only keep it in.
- If grease or cooking oil catches fire, throw baking soda or salt at the bottom of the flame to put it out. (Water will *not* put out a grease fire.) Call for help, and try to turn all the stove burners to "off."

Cooking Utensils

colander—A bowl with holes in the bottom and sides. It is used for draining liquid from a solid food.

double boiler—A utensil made up of two pans that fit together. Heat from the water boiling in the lower pan cooks food in the upper pan without scorching.

Dutch oven—A heavy pot, with a tight-fitting domed lid, that is often used for cooking soups or stews

slotted spoon—A spoon with small openings in the bowl. It is often used to pick solid food out of a liquid.

Cooking Terms

baste—To pour or spoon liquid over food as it roasts in order to flavor and moisten it

boil—To heat a liquid over high heat until bubbles form and rise rapidly to the surface

core—To remove the center part of a fruit or vegetable, which contains the stem and/or seeds

cream—To beat one or several ingredients to a smooth consistency

florets—Individual, flowerlike pieces that form the heads of such vegetables as cauliflower and broccoli

fold—To blend an ingredient with other ingredients by using a gentle overturning circular motion instead of by stirring or beating

grate—To shred food into small pieces by rubbing it against a grater

knead—To work dough by pressing it with the palms, pushing it outward, and then pressing it over on itself

pinch—A very small amount, usually what you can pick up between your thumb and forefinger *preheat*—To allow an oven to warm up to a certain temperature before putting food in it

shred—To tear or cut food into tiny pieces, either by hand or by using a knife or grater

simmer—To cook over low heat in liquid kept just below its boiling point. Bubbles may occasionally rise to the surface.

whip—To beat a substance such as cream, gelatin, or egg white at high speed until light and fluffy in texture

Special Ingredients

allspice—The berry of a West Indian tree. It is used whole or ground in cooking to give a slightly sweet flavor to food.

almond extract—A liquid made from almonds that is used in baking

bay leaves—The dried leaves of the bay (also called laurel) tree

bread crumbs—Tiny pieces of stale or dried bread made by crushing the bread with the bottom of a glass or a rolling pin. Packaged bread crumbs can be bought at grocery stores.

cinnamon—A spice made from the bark of a tree in the laurel family. Cinnamon is available ground and in sticks.

cloves—Dried buds from a small evergreen tree. Cloves can be used either whole or ground to flavor food.

Dijon-style mustard—A commercially prepared condiment made from mustard seed, white wine, vinegar, salt, and spices

dill—An herb whose seeds and leaves are both used in cooking. Dried dill is also called dill weed.

dried mushrooms—Fresh mushrooms that have been dried. They have a leathery texture and are usually used in soups or other foods in which they can soak up liquid.

garlic—An herb whose distinctive flavor is used in many dishes. Fresh garlic can usually be found in the produce department of a supermarket. Each piece or bulb can be broken up into several small sections called cloves. Most recipes use only one or two finely chopped cloves of this very strong herb. Before you chop up a clove of garlic, you will have to remove the brittle, papery covering that surrounds it.

kohlrabi—A light-green vegetable in the turnip family

marjoram—An herb related to mint that is used in cooking. It is known for its sweet aroma and flavor.

paprika—A seasoning made from dried, ground sweet red peppers, used for its flavor and its red color

parsley—A green, leafy herb used as a seasoning and as a garnish

parsnip—The long, white, sweet-tasting root vegetable of the parsnip plant

pearl barley—Seeds of the barley plant that have been rubbed into smooth, round grains. Pearl barley is usually used in soups and ground-meat dishes.

peppercorns—The berries of an East Indian plant. Peppercorns are used both whole and ground to flavor food.

poppy seed pastry filling—A thick, sweet mixture made from poppy seeds and corn syrup that is used in making pies, cakes, and breads

rutabaga—An edible, yellowish root vegetable similar to the turnip

sauerkraut—A strongly flavored fermented mixture of shredded cabbage, salt, and spices

vanilla extract—A liquid made from vanilla beans and used to flavor food

white-wine vinegar—Vinegar made from white wine. It has a sharp, tangy flavor.

Healthy and Low-Fat Cooking Tips

Many modern cooks are concerned about preparing healthy, low-fat meals. Fortunately, there are simple ways to reduce the fat content of most dishes. Here are a few general tips for adapting the recipes in this book. Throughout the book, you'll also find specific suggestions for individual recipes—and don't worry, they'll still taste delicious!

Many recipes call for butter or oil to sauté vegetables or other ingredients. Using oil lowers saturated fat right away, but you can also reduce the amount of oil you use. You can also substitute a low-fat or nonfat cooking spray for oil. Sprinkling a little salt on vegetables brings out their natural juices, so less oil is needed. It's also a good idea to use a small, nonstick frying pan if you decide to use less oil than the recipe calls for.

Another common substitution for butter is margarine. Before making this substitution, consider the recipe. If it is a dessert, it's often best to use butter. Margarine may noticeably change the taste or consistency of the food.

Dairy products, such as cream, milk, and sour cream, are common in Polish cooking. An easy way to trim fat from a recipe is to use skim or evaporated skim milk in place of cream, whole milk, or 2 percent milk. In recipes that call for sour cream, you may want to try substituting low-fat or nonfat sour cream or plain yogurt.

Some cooks like to replace ground beef with ground turkey to lower fat. However, since this does change the flavor, you may need to experiment a little bit to decide if you like this substitution. Buying extra-lean meats is always an easy way to reduce fat.

There are many ways to prepare meals that are good for you and still taste great. As you become a more experienced cook, try experimenting with recipes and substitutions to find the methods that work best for you.

METRIC CONVERSIONS

Cooks in the United States measure both liquid and solid ingredients using standard containers based on the 8-ounce cup and the tablespoon. These measurements are based on volume, while the metric system of measurement is based on both weight (for solids) and volume (for liquids). To convert from U.S. fluid tablespoons, ounces, quarts, and so forth to metric liters is a straightforward conversion, using the chart below. However, since solids have different weights—one cup of rice does not weigh the same as one cup of grated cheese, for example—many cooks who use the metric system have kitchen scales to weigh different ingredients. The chart below will give you a good starting point for basic conversions to the metric system.

MASS (weight)

1 ounce (oz.)	=	28.0 grams (g)
8 ounces	=	227.0 grams
1 pound (lb.) or 16 ounces	=	0.45 kilograms (kg)
2.2 pounds	=	1.0 kilogram

LIQUID VOLUME

1 teaspoon (tsp.)	=	5.0 milliliters (ml)
1 tablespoon (tbsp.)	=	15.0 milliliters
1 fluid ounce (oz.)	=	30.0 milliliters
1 cup (c.)	=	240 milliliters
1 pint (pt.)	=	480 milliliters
1 quart (qt.)	=	0.95 liters (l)
1 gallon (gal.)	=	3.80 liters

LENGTH

¼ inch (in.)	=	0.6 centimeters (cm)
½ inch	=	1.25 centimeters
1 inch	=	2.5 centimeters

TEMPERATURE

212°F	=	100°C (boiling point of water)
225°F	=	110°C
250°F	=	120°C
275°F	=	135°C
300°F	=	150°C
325°F	=	160°C
350°F	=	180°C
375°F	=	190°C
400°F	=	200°C

(To convert temperature in Fahrenheit to Celsius, subtract 32 and multiply by .56)

PAN SIZES

8-inch cake pan	=	20 x 4-centimeter cake pan
9-inch cake pan	=	23 x 3.5-centimeter cake pan
11 x 7-inch baking pan	=	28 x 18-centimeter baking pan
13 x 9-inch baking pan	=	32.5 x 23-centimeter baking pan
9 x 5-inch loaf pan	=	23 x 13-centimeter loaf pan
2-quart casserole	=	2-liter casserole

A Polish Table

A Polish table reflects the importance of mealtime in Poland. It is always pleasant to look at and is an enjoyable place to sit down. Linen tablecloths or handmade place mats are used along with cloth napkins and simple place settings of silverware. A centerpiece of freshly cut flowers is often on the table, and, for special occasions, a small vase of flowers is put at each place.

For most meals, food is placed in china serving dishes that are passed from person to person and then placed in the center of the table. For larger, more formal dinners, the food is often served buffet style. Several condiments are commonly found on Polish tables, including salt, pepper, and horseradish. Fresh-fruit compote is often included on the dinner table to accompany the main dish.

A Polish family sits down to afternoon tea.

A Polish Menu

Below are menu plans for a typical, hearty Polish dinner and light supper, along with shopping lists of the items necessary to prepare these meals. The combinations of dishes below are only suggestions. As you gain more experience cooking Polish meals, you will discover the menu plans that you like best.

DINNER

Bread

Tomato and onion
tier salad

Rutabagas and carrots

Pierożki

Roast stuffed fish

SHOPPING LIST:

Produce

3 medium tomatoes
3 small onions
1 large rutabaga
6–8 medium carrots
½ lb. fresh mushrooms
fresh parsley

Dairy/Egg/Meat

8 oz. cottage cheese
1 stick butter or margarine
4 oz. sour cream
½ pint skim milk
½ pint half and half
4 eggs
4 to 6 skinned fish fillets

Canned/Bottled/Boxed

4 oz. sauerkraut (available in
cans or jars)

Miscellaneous

1 loaf bread
bread crumbs
flour
sugar
dill weed
paprika
marjoram
garlic powder
salt
pepper

SUPPER

Bread with cheese

Cabbage rolls

Semi-short bread with plums

Tea with lemon

SHOPPING LIST:

Produce

1 onion
1 small head cabbage
1 bulb garlic
1 lb. purple plums or
    apricots
1 lemon

Dairy/Egg/Meat

assorted cheeses
8 oz. sour cream
1 stick butter or margarine
3 eggs
½ lb. lean ground beef
¼ lb. lean ground pork

Canned/Bottled/Boxed

6 oz. tomato paste
12 oz. canned tomato juice
vegetable or olive oil
baking powder
vanilla or almond extract
rice or pearl barley
tea

Miscellaneous

1 loaf bread
flour
sugar
powdered sugar
oregano
dried parsley
basil
cayenne pepper
salt
pepper

Breakfast and Second Breakfast

Breakfast in Poland is a hearty, filling meal, especially in the winter when it's snowy and cold. Usually eaten between 6:00 and 8:00 A.M., a Polish breakfast gives people the energy they need to start the day. In the winter, oatmeal or hot wheat cereal is usually served along with bread and butter, bagels and cream cheese, sliced meats, and mild cheeses. Summertime breakfasts are usually a bit lighter, consisting of bagels and cream cheese, croissants and jam, bread and butter, and sliced meats and cheeses.

Between 11:00 A.M. and 1:00 P.M., a second breakfast is eaten by people who have only a short break from work and by schoolchildren. Those who have a longer break at midday often go home or eat in a milk bar, a restaurant that offers only meatless, milk-based dishes. Second breakfast may consist of an open-face sandwich, hot homemade soup or stew, a raw or marinated vegetable, and fruit.

Mushrooms, potatoes, and carrots make this simple barley soup a perfect autumn dish. (Recipe on page 32.)

Barley Soup / Krupnik

This hearty soup is easy to adapt according to your personal tastes and what you have on hand. Try adding celery, corn, peas, or other veggies for extra variety.

1 medium potato

1 carrot

4 10¾-oz. cans (about 6 cups) beef or vegetable broth

½ tbsp. dried parsley flakes

½ tbsp. dill weed

2 or 3 fresh mushrooms

1 tsp. butter or margarine

¼ c. pearl barley

1. Peel potato and carrot and cut into bite-sized pieces.

2. Put all but ¾ c. broth into a large kettle. Add potato, carrot, parsley flakes, and dill weed and bring to a boil. Reduce heat to low and cover.

3. Meanwhile, clean and slice mushrooms. Melt butter in a skillet over medium heat. Add barley and mushrooms and sauté 1 to 2 minutes. Add remaining broth and simmer 5 to 7 minutes, or until mushrooms are soft.

4. Add barley mixture to kettle and simmer for about 45 minutes, or until barley is tender.

5. Serve hot.*

Preparation time: 10 minutes
Cooking time: 1 ¼ hours
Serves 4 to 6

For a special treat, stir in ¼ c. evaporated skim milk just before serving. This makes a rich and creamy soup that is still low in fat.

Mushrooms in Vinegar / Grzybki w Occie

This popular dish is made with very fresh mushrooms in Poland, where people often pick their own in the country's many forests.

2 c. white-wine vinegar

3 tbsp. sugar

¼ tsp. whole peppercorns

¼ tsp. whole allspice

1 whole clove garlic

2 bay leaves

2 lb. fresh mushrooms

1 small onion

6 c. water

1 tsp. salt

1. Put vinegar, sugar, peppercorns, allspice, garlic, and bay leaves in a saucepan. Bring to a boil, then remove from heat and cool.

2. Clean mushrooms and trim off ends. (Do not remove whole stem.) Peel onion.

3. Put 6 c. water and the salt in a large saucepan and bring to a boil. Add mushrooms and whole onion and boil 3 to 4 minutes. Remove from heat, drain through a colander, and let cool.

4. Put 3 tbsp. vinegar mixture into each of 2 qt. jars. Divide mushrooms equally and put into jars. Slice boiled onion and place equal amounts on top of mushrooms in each jar. Fill each jar with remaining vinegar mixture. Cover and refrigerate until ready to serve.*

*If covered tightly, mushrooms in vinegar will keep for up to two months in the refrigerator.

Preparation time: 20 minutes
Cooking time: 25 to 30 minutes
Makes 2 quarts

Hunter's Stew/*Bigos*

Hunter's stew has been the Polish national dish for hundreds of years. This tempting stew can be eaten hot or cold. It is delicious when reheated, and the leftovers can be frozen for future use.

1 16-oz. jar or can sauerkraut

½ c. (1 stick) butter or margarine

2 dried mushrooms, crushed (optional)

½ tsp. salt

1 tsp. black pepper

1 tsp. marjoram

1 tsp. dried parsley flakes

1 tsp. basil

⅛ tsp. cayenne pepper (optional)

2 tbsp. paprika

2 or 3 cloves garlic, minced

1 6-oz. can tomato paste

1 tbsp. sugar

6 to 8 pitted, dried prunes

1 small head cabbage

2 large green apples

2 carrots

1. Preheat oven to 325°F.

2. Place sauerkraut in colander to drain. Using your hands, squeeze out any remaining liquid. Chop sauerkraut into smaller pieces.

3. Melt ¼ c. butter or margarine in a large skillet. Add sauerkraut, mushrooms, salt, pepper, marjoram, parsley, basil, cayenne, paprika, garlic, tomato paste, and sugar and sauté for 10 minutes over medium heat. Remove from heat and set aside.

4. Chop prunes into small pieces. Core, wash, and shred cabbage. Peel, core, and chop apples into bite-sized pieces. Peel and grate carrots. Peel and chop tomatoes and onion into small pieces.

5. Place water and all ingredients from step 4 in a Dutch oven. Cover and put on middle oven rack to begin cooking.

2 medium tomatoes

1 medium onion

5 c. water

½ lb. each boneless stewing beef, pork, and venison*

½ lb. each smoked ham and smoked Polish sausage

½ c. all-purpose flour

*In Poland, venison is commonly used in hunter's stew, but if it's not available you can substitute ½ lb. of beef or an additional ¼ lb. each of beef and pork. For a vegetarian stew, you can leave out the meat entirely and add extra vegetables instead.

6. Cut all meat into bite-sized pieces. Put flour into a clean paper bag. Place cubes of meat (except ham and Polish sausage) into bag, about ¼ lb. at a time, and shake to coat meat.

7. Melt remaining ¼ c. butter or margarine in a large skillet or heavy pot and brown meat (except ham and sausage) on all sides over medium-high heat.

8. Add meat, ham and sausage, and sauerkraut mixture from step 3 to Dutch oven and mix well.

9. Return stew to oven and cook for 2 to 2½ hours, or until meat is tender.

10. Serve stew hot in individual bowls along with bread, mashed potatoes, or rice.

Preparation time: 25 to 35 minutes
Cooking time: 2½ to 3 hours
Serves 8 to 10

Dinner

Dinner is the main meal of the day in Poland and is not eaten until early evening, usually between 4:30 and 6:00 P.M. Anyone who feels a bit hungry before then might take the opportunity to enjoy a cup of tea and a snack. Many Poles like to take some time in the afternoon to go to a teashop, where people gather for refreshment and lively conversation. Tea is served steaming hot in tall, thin glasses with sugar and a slice of lemon floating on top. Coffee is served in demitasse cups and sometimes topped with whipped cream. The best part of this snack, though, is eating one of the wonderful Polish pastries that are baked fresh daily.

By dinnertime, all of the family members are home from work and school. The Polish people have very strong family ties, so this meal is especially important. It is the time of the day when each family member can share the day's events with the others. At a Polish dinner table, one can always find friendly conversation, family togetherness, and mouth-watering food.

Vegetable salad (top) and tomato and onion tier salad (bottom left) *add a fresh taste to your table. (Recipes on pages 38 and 39.)*

Vegetable Salad / Sałatka z Jarzyn

White beans lend flavor and texture to this nutritious, great-tasting salad. You can use any kind of cooked white bean including navy, great northern, or small white. This salad is best when chilled in the refrigerator (covered) for at least one hour before serving.

1 large potato

2 carrots, peeled

½ lb. fresh or frozen green peas

1 parsnip, peeled

1 tart apple, cored and chopped

1 dill pickle, chopped

1 8-oz. can cooked white beans, drained

½ c. mayonnaise*

1 tsp. Dijon-style mustard

lettuce leaves

1 or 2 hard-cooked eggs, cut into 4 wedges each (make 1 crosswise and 1 lengthwise cut in each)

*To reduce fat in this salad, try using low-fat or nonfat mayonnaise or replace the mayonnaise with plain yogurt.

1. Boil potato in skin about 20 minutes, or until tender but not mushy, then chill.

2. In three separate saucepans, boil carrots, peas, and parsnip until tender. If necessary, cut carrots and parsnip in half to fit in pans. Drain and chill. (Boil carrots about 15 minutes, parsnip about 10 minutes, and peas about 5 minutes, or according to directions on package.)

3. Chop carrots and parsnip into bite-sized pieces. Peel and chop potato.

4. In a large bowl, mix cooked vegetables, apple, pickle, and canned beans with mayonnaise and mustard.

5. To serve, arrange salad on lettuce leaves on individual salad plates. Garnish with hard-cooked egg wedges. (See page 40 for directions for hard cooking eggs.)

Preparation time: 35 to 45 minutes
Cooking time: 45 to 55 minutes
(plus 25 to 30 minutes for eggs)
Serves 4 to 6

Tomato and Onion Tier Salad/
Sałatka z Pomidorów z Cebulą

This salad takes only a few minutes to prepare, but it's a perfectly refreshing combination of tastes and textures.

3 medium tomatoes*

2 small onions

salt

pepper

dill weed

1. Wash and core the tomatoes. Cut into thin slices.

2. Peel onions and cut into thin slices.

3. Lay tomato slices side by side on a platter. Place one onion slice on top of each tomato slice. Continue to make layers of tomatoes and onions until all are used up.

4. Sprinkle lightly with salt, pepper, and dill weed and serve.

Preparation time: 15 to 20 minutes
Serves 4 to 6

*Try adding thinly sliced cucumbers to this salad for extra color and variety.

Eggs Stuffed with Ham/
Jajka Nadziewane Szynką

The leftovers of the delicious filling can be used as sandwich spread or for making pierożki.

4 hard-cooked eggs

½ lb. cooked ham*

¼ c. grated Monterey Jack cheese*

4 tbsp. sour cream*

2 tsp. Dijon-style mustard

⅛ tsp. pepper

parsley or dill

1. Hard cook eggs by placing in a saucepan and covering with cold water. Place over medium heat until water boils, reduce heat, and simmer for 15 minutes. Drain water from saucepan and run cold water over eggs until they are cool.

2. Peel eggs. Cut in half lengthwise and remove but do not discard yolks. Cut off a small slice of the rounded part of each egg half so they will sit flat on a plate.

3. Chop ham into very small pieces.

4. Blend ham, cheese, egg yolks, sour cream, mustard, and pepper with a fork.

5. Stuff each egg half with ham mixture. Arrange on a serving plate and top each egg with a sprig of parsley or a sprinkling of dill.

Preparation time: 25 to 30 minutes
Cooking time: 25 minutes
Makes 8 stuffed eggs

To lower the fat content of this creamy dish, trim all fat from the ham and use low-fat or nonfat cheese and sour cream. For meatless eggs, leave out the ham altogether.

Pierożki

Pierożki are an old Polish favorite. They can be filled with potatoes, meat, mushrooms, or almost anything else a creative cook might want to try. Fill half of your pierożki with the sauerkraut mixture and half with the cheese filling for a tasty selection.

Sauerkraut Filling:

4 oz. sauerkraut, drained

2 tbsp. butter or margarine

½ onion, peeled and chopped

¼ tsp. paprika

¼ tsp. salt

¼ tsp. pepper

¼ tsp. marjoram

1. Chop sauerkraut into very small pieces.
2. Melt butter or margarine in skillet. Add sauerkraut and remaining ingredients and fry over low heat for about 10 minutes, stirring occasionally.
3. Fill and cook pierożki as directed.

Preparation time: 15 to 20 minutes

Savory Cheese Filling:

8 oz. (1 c.) cottage cheese

2 tbsp. bread crumbs

1 egg yolk

½ tsp. salt

¼ tsp. pepper

pinch of garlic powder (optional)

1. Put all ingredients in a medium bowl and mix well.
2. Fill and cook pierożki as directed.

Preparation time: 5 to 10 minutes

Dough:

2 c. all-purpose flour

1 egg

⅛ tsp. salt

½ to ¾ c. water or skim milk

extra flour for mixing

1 tsp. salt

1. In a medium bowl, mix together flour, egg, and ⅛ tsp. salt. Mix in water or milk, a little at a time, until dough is stiff.

2. Knead dough for 2 to 4 minutes on a floured surface. (You will probably have to add more flour.) Roll out dough to ⅛-inch thickness with a rolling pin.

3. With a drinking glass or cookie cutter, cut out rounds of dough 3 inches in diameter.

4. Put 1 tbsp. of either filling on one half of a dough circle.

5. Moisten edges of dough with a little water. Fold dough over filling and press edges together, first with your fingers, then with the tines of a fork. Repeat with remaining dough and filling.

6. Fill a large kettle with water and 1 tsp. salt and bring to boil. Place pieroźki in boiling water a few at a time. (If you put too many in the kettle at once, they will stick together.) Boil for 3 to 5 minutes, or until pieroźki begin to float.

7. Serve hot, with sour cream if desired.

Preparation time: 40 to 50 minutes
Cooking time: 45 minutes to 1 hour
Makes 12 to 18 pieroźki

Rutabagas and Carrots/
Brukiew z Marchwią Zasmażana

Rutabagas make this a filling side dish, perfect for a chilly autumn evening.

1 large rutabaga*

6 to 8 medium carrots

4 c. water

1 tsp. salt

3 tbsp. butter or margarine, softened

2 tsp. all-purpose flour

1 tbsp. sugar

1 tbsp. chopped fresh parsley or 1 tsp. dried parsley flakes

½ tsp. salt

1. Peel rutabaga and carrots and cut into bite-sized pieces.

2. In a large saucepan, bring water and salt to a boil.

3. Add vegetables and cook about 15 to 20 minutes, or until tender but not mushy.

4. Meanwhile, blend butter, flour, sugar, parsley, and salt with a fork. Melt butter mixture in skillet over medium heat.

5. Drain vegetables and place in a bowl. Pour sauce over vegetables, mix well, and serve steaming hot.

Preparation time: 20 minutes
Cooking time: 30 to 40 minutes
Serves 4 to 6

*Rutabagas are available at most supermarkets year-round. Look for rutabagas that are smooth skinned, firm to the touch, and heavy for their size.

This vegetable dish is simple to prepare and can be made with a variety of root vegetables such as potatoes, parsnips, and yams.

Cauliflower with Polish Sauce/
Kalafior w Sosie Polskim

Polish sauce is an easy but flavorful topping that is delicious with a wide variety of vegetables. Polish cooks might serve it over carrots, cabbage, green beans, asparagus, or brussels sprouts.

1 medium head cauliflower*

Polish Sauce:

2 tbsp. butter or margarine

2 tbsp. bread crumbs

½ tsp. dill weed

*When buying fresh cauliflower, choose heads that are firm and very white, with crisp, green leaves. To store cauliflower for a couple of days, cover the whole head with plastic wrap and put it in the refrigerator.

1. Remove any green leaves from cauliflower and trim stem. Wash under cool running water. Place whole cauliflower right side up in a large kettle. Put enough water in the kettle to reach bottom florets (the ones closest to the stem) of the cauliflower and add ½ tsp. salt to the water. Cover the kettle tightly and bring water to a boil. Cook cauliflower for about 12 to 15 minutes, or until tender but not mushy.

2. In a small frying pan, melt butter over medium heat until it sizzles. (Butter burns easily, so be careful not to let it turn brown.) Add bread crumbs and dill weed and stir until mixture is golden brown.

3. When cauliflower is cooked, transfer to a serving platter. Top cauliflower with Polish sauce and serve right away by carefully cutting off pieces with a serving spoon.

Preparation time: 5 to 10 minutes
Cooking time: 20 to 30 minutes
Serves 4 to 6

Roast Stuffed Fish / *Ryba Nadziewana Pieczona*

4 to 6 skinned fish fillets*

2 tsp. butter or margarine

Stuffing:

1 tbsp. butter or margarine, softened

2 eggs, separated

½ lb. fresh mushrooms, sliced

4 or 5 tbsp. bread crumbs

½ tsp. salt

¼ tsp. pepper

Sauce:

½ c. half and half

½ c. sour cream

¼ tsp. salt

*For this dish, most Polish cooks stuff a whole fish—usually a carp or other white fish. This simple version, using any white fish fillet (such as halibut or cod) is just as delicious.

1. In a mixing bowl, cream together butter and egg yolks with a fork. In another bowl, beat the egg whites with an egg beater or fork until foamy and add to yolks. Mix in mushrooms, bread crumbs, salt, and pepper.

2. Place some stuffing in the center of each fillet, dividing it evenly among the fillets. Roll up fillets and use toothpicks to hold in place.

3. Preheat oven to 350°F. Grease the bottom of glass baking dish.

4. Melt 2 tsp. butter in saucepan. Place fillet rolls seam-side-down in baking dish with any extra stuffing. Pour melted butter over fish.

5. Put dish on middle oven rack and bake uncovered 40 minutes, basting frequently with drippings from fish. (If liquid in dish dries up, sprinkle fish with water.)

6. Stir half and half into sour cream, a little at a time, until smooth. Add salt and mix well. Pour sauce over fish and bake 5 minutes longer.

7. Remove fish and extra stuffing to serving plate and serve hot.

Preparation time: 25 to 30 minutes
Cooking time: 45 minutes
Serves 4 to 6

Supper

A Polish supper is eaten at about 8:00 P.M., not too long after dinner. And, since bedtime may not be too far off, especially for children, this is a much lighter meal than dinner. It usually consists of bread and cheese, a light main course that might be either hot or cold, a side dish of marinated vegetables, and sometimes dessert.

After supper, the family might sit around the table to enjoy some leisurely conversation or perhaps a game. Children and adults alike drink hot tea with lemon or honey as they relax at the end of the day.

A dish of cabbage rolls (bottom), served with semi-short bread with plums (top) for dessert, makes a satisfying evening meal. (Recipes on pages 54–55 and 56–57.)

Plum and Rhubarb Soup/
Zupa Śliwkowo Rabarbarowa

This delicious soup can be eaten either hot at the beginning of a meal or cold for dessert.

½ lb. plums*

½ lb. rhubarb*

6 c. water

3 or 4 whole cloves

1 1-inch stick cinnamon

¼ c. sugar

¼ c. cold water

2 tbsp. all-purpose flour or
cornstarch

½ c. sour cream

*Dried, pitted prunes can be used instead of
plums in this recipe, and tart green apples
can be substituted for rhubarb. If you use
apples, peel and core them. If you use prunes,
cover them with water and soak overnight.
The liquid can then be used in the soup.*

1. Wash fruit. Remove pits from plums. Remove ends and tops of rhubarb. Chop fruit into chunks.

2. Combine fruit, water, cloves, cinnamon, and sugar in a large kettle. Bring to a boil, then cover, reduce heat, and simmer for 10 to 15 minutes.

3. Remove cloves and cinnamon with a slotted spoon and discard. Then carefully remove half of fruit with slotted spoon and place in a large mixing bowl. Mash well with a fork.

4. In a cup, gradually add ¼ c. cold water to flour or cornstarch to make a thick paste.

5. Add paste to the mashed fruit and return fruit to kettle. As soon as soup begins to boil, remove from heat and let stand for 3 or 4 minutes.

6. Serve soup hot or cold with dollops of sour cream on top.

Preparation time: 20 to 30 minutes
Cooking time: 45 to 60 minutes
Serves 6 to 8

Cabbage Rolls / Gołabki

Gołabki translates literally as "little pigeons." Once these cabbage rolls are nestled in a casserole dish, it isn't hard to see where they got their name!

Filling:

⅓ c. uncooked white or brown rice or pearl barley

½ lb. ground beef*

¼ lb. ground pork*

1 egg, lightly beaten

1 medium onion, chopped

½ tsp. oregano

½ tsp. dried parsley flakes

½ tsp. basil

½ tsp. salt

¼ tsp. pepper

Wrapping:

1 small head cabbage

1. Cook rice or barley according to directions on package.

2. In a large mixing bowl, combine cooked rice or barley, ground beef, pork, egg, half of the chopped onion, oregano, parsley, basil, salt, and pepper and mix well.

3. Core and wash the cabbage and place in a large kettle of boiling, salted water for 10 minutes, or until outer leaves become tender. Carefully remove cabbage from water with tongs, cool a bit, and pull off the tender outer leaves without tearing them. When you reach a layer of crisp leaves, return cabbage to boiling water until leaves become tender. Repeat this process until you have pulled off 10 to 15 whole cabbage leaves.

4. In a mixing bowl, combine tomato paste, flour, sugar, remaining onion, pepper, oregano, parsley, basil, cayenne, and garlic. Mix well. Add tomato juice, a little at a time, and stir until smooth. Continue stirring and add the oil.

Sauce:

1 6-oz. can tomato paste

1 tbsp. all-purpose flour

1½ tsp. sugar

½ tsp. pepper

½ tsp. oregano

½ tsp. dried parsley flakes

½ tsp. basil

pinch of cayenne pepper (optional)

1 clove garlic, minced

1 12-oz. can tomato or cocktail
   vegetable juice

1½ tsp. olive or vegetable oil

**Make a delicious meatless
version of this dish by replacing
the beef and pork with an extra
½ c. rice (uncooked) and ½ lb. fresh
mushrooms, diced and sautéed. Diced
boiled potatoes also make a
good substitution.*

5. Cut large cabbage leaves lengthwise on both sides of heavy center vein and discard vein. You should end up with about 20 cabbage wrappings.

6. Place 1 tbsp. filling at one end of a cabbage leaf. Roll up leaf and bend slightly to form a crescent-shaped roll. Repeat with remaining leaves and filling.

7. Preheat oven to 375°F.

8. Put ½ c. sauce into a deep casserole dish with a lid.

9. Place cabbage rolls side by side in the dish, making sure they fit together tightly. Make two layers of rolls, pouring a little more sauce between layers. (Do not fill casserole dish more than halfway up the sides.) Pour remaining sauce over the top.

10. Cover casserole dish tightly. Place dish on the middle oven rack and bake for 30 minutes.

11. Uncover dish and bake 20 to 25 minutes more.

12. Serve from the casserole dish, spooning plenty of sauce over each helping.

Preparation time: 1 to 1¼ hours
(plus 25 to 30 minutes for rice or barley)
Cooking time: 55 to 65 minutes
Makes about 20 cabbage rolls

Semi-Short Bread with Plums/
Placek Półkruchy ze Śliwkami

Purple plums and a sprinkling of powdered sugar make this dessert a treat for the eyes and for the taste buds.

Topping:

1 lb. fresh purple plums*

¼ c. powdered sugar

½ c. sour cream

1 tsp. vanilla or almond extract

1. Preheat oven to 375°F.

2. Grease and flour a 9 × 13-inch baking pan.

3. Wash plums, cut in half lengthwise, and remove pits.

4. In a mixing bowl, make topping by blending together powdered sugar, sour cream, and vanilla or almond extract.

5. In another bowl, combine flour, baking powder, powdered sugar, and salt.

6. Cut butter into small pieces and add to flour mixture. Blend with a fork until mixture resembles large bread crumbs.

For a variation on this recipe, substitute apricots, apples, or pears for plums.

Dough:

2 c. all-purpose flour

1½ tsp. baking powder

½ c. powdered sugar

½ tsp. salt

4 tbsp. (½ stick) butter or
    margarine, softened

1 egg, lightly beaten

1 egg yolk

4 oz. (½ c.) sour cream

¼ to ½ c. powdered sugar for
    sprinkling

7. Add egg, egg yolk, and sour cream to flour mixture and mix well with your hands until smooth.

8. Spread dough evenly on bottom of baking pan.

9. Place plum halves skin-side-down on dough and press into dough. (Make sure there is some dough showing around each plum.) Put 1 tsp. topping on each plum half.

10. Put on middle oven rack and bake 30 minutes, or until golden brown.

11. Put powdered sugar in flour sifter and sift over top. Cut into squares to serve.

Preparation time: 45 to 60 minutes
Cooking time: 30 minutes
Makes 18 to 24 squares

Vegetable Bouquet/*Bukiet z Jarzyn*

Fresh green and yellow beans will add flavor and a slight crunch to this dish. If fresh beans are not available, however, you can use 8 oz. each of frozen beans instead. Cook the beans according to package directions and drain well before using.

1 lb. new potatoes

½ lb. fresh green beans

½ lb. fresh yellow beans

½ lb. baby carrots

½ medium head cauliflower

2 slices white bread

Polish sauce (recipe on p. 47)

1. Wash all fresh vegetables. If you are using fresh beans, trim off ends and leave beans whole. Leave carrots whole. Wash cauliflower and cut into florets. Boil each vegetable in a separate saucepan until crisp yet tender. (Boil potatoes about 20 minutes, carrots and cauliflower about 10 to 15 minutes each, and beans about 5 minutes.)

2. Prepare a double portion of Polish sauce.

3. Toast bread and cut into 2-inch strips.

4. Drain all vegetables. Arrange on a large serving platter, separating each type of vegetable from the next with a strip of toast.

5. Top vegetables with Polish sauce and serve immediately.

Preparation time: 30 minutes
(plus 15 minutes for Polish sauce)
Cooking time: 25 to 30 minutes
Serves 6

Holiday and Festival Food

A Polish celebration or holiday gathering of any kind wouldn't seem complete without at least a sampling of festive foods. Polish cooks, young and old, often rely on traditional family recipes that have been passed down for generations. But each cook also adds his or her special touches to the meal, creating new variations and traditions over the years.

The recipes in this section will give you a taste of the many delicious customs that help to make Polish holidays and festivals such a treat. Although most of these dishes are associated with specific occasions, you can prepare them anytime to turn an ordinary meal into a special event.

Colorful Christmas Eve borscht (top) *and herring paste with bread* (bottom) *offer a delicious taste of the holidays in Poland. (Recipes on pages 62 and 63.)*

Christmas Eve Borscht*/Wigilijny Barszcz

Borscht is one of the most traditional soups in Polish cuisine, and many cooks serve a meatless borscht such as this one at the Christmas Eve feast.

32 oz. canned red beets, diced

3 c. water

1 medium stalk celery, chopped

2 carrots, peeled and cut into 2-inch pieces

1 medium onion, peeled and thickly sliced

¼ tsp. whole peppercorns

¼ tsp. salt

1 tsp. vinegar

1 tbsp. lemon juice

1 tsp. sugar

dash of garlic powder

salt and pepper to taste

sour cream and fresh dill to garnish

1. Drain beets and save the liquid. Set beets aside. In a large saucepan, combine beet liquid, water, celery, carrots, onion, peppercorns, and salt.

2. Bring to a boil. Reduce heat, cover, and simmer 15 to 20 minutes.

3. Carefully use a slotted spoon to remove and discard celery, carrots, onion, and peppercorns.

4. Add beets, vinegar, lemon juice, sugar, and garlic powder. Simmer uncovered for 10 minutes, or until heated through. Add salt and pepper to taste and serve hot with sour cream and dill.

Preparation time: 10 minutes
Cooking time: 25 to 40 minutes
Serves 6 to 8

*To add something extra to this festive borscht, try preparing some simple dumplings. In a medium mixing bowl, combine 1½ c. flour, 1 egg, ¾ c. water, and a dash of salt. Beat well for 2 minutes. Drop teaspoonfuls of dough into boiling water and cook until dumplings float. Add to hot soup and serve!

Herring Paste on Bread/
Kanapki z Pasty Śledziowej

This strongly flavored spread is just one of many delicious appetizers that might be served at a typical Polish New Year's Eve party.

2 eggs

1 8-oz. jar marinated herring fillets, drained (any kind)

¼ c. butter or margarine, softened

fresh dill to garnish

1 loaf rye or pumpernickel bread

1. Hard cook eggs by placing in a saucepan and covering with cold water. Place over medium heat until boiling, reduce heat, and simmer for 15 minutes. Drain water from saucepan and run cold water over eggs until they are cool.

2. Peel cooked eggs. Cut in half lengthwise and remove yolks (but do not discard).

3. Put herring, hard-cooked egg yolks, and butter in blender and blend until smooth.*

4. Spoon herring into serving dish. Garnish with pieces of hard-cooked egg white and sprigs of dill and serve with thinly sliced rye or pumpernickel bread.

Preparation time: 15 minutes
Cooking time: 25 minutes
Makes 1½ cups

If you don't have a blender, cut herring into very small pieces and place in a bowl. Add egg yolks and butter and mash well with a fork.

Noodles with Poppy Seeds/ *Kluski z Makiem*

In Poland, this wonderful dish is traditionally eaten only on Christmas Eve. It is just one of up to twelve courses served after a day of fasting.

16 oz. egg noodles

1 12½-oz. can poppy seed pastry filling

4 tbsp. honey

1 c. heavy cream or half and half

½ c. golden raisins*

2 tbsp. butter or margarine

1. Cook noodles in boiling water, following directions on package.

2. Meanwhile, combine poppy seed filling, honey, and cream in a mixing bowl and stir until smooth. Stir in raisins.

3. Melt butter in double boiler or a medium-sized saucepan. Add poppy seed mixture and heat thoroughly.

4. Pour poppy seed mixture over hot, drained noodles and serve immediately.

Preparation and cooking time: 20 to 30 minutes
Serves 10 to 12

*Golden raisins are made from the same kind of grapes as dark raisins but are generally larger and juicier. Look for golden raisins at your local supermarket.

Poppy seeds are an old favorite in Poland, where fields bloom with bright poppies every year.

Honey Cake / *Piernik*

Polish hosts and hostesses often offer a slice of this delicious dessert to lucky holiday guests.

8 tbsp. (1 stick) butter

4 eggs, separated

1½ c. honey

3 c. all-purpose flour

½ tsp. ground ginger

½ tsp. nutmeg

½ tsp. ground cloves

1 tsp. cinnamon

2 tsp. baking powder

1. Preheat oven to 350°F.

2. In a large mixing bowl, cream butter by beating until soft and smooth. Add egg yolks one at a time and beat well.

3. Add honey and mix well.

4. In a medium mixing bowl, sift together flour, ginger, nutmeg, cloves, cinnamon, and baking powder. Add to butter mixture and mix well.

5. In a medium mixing bowl, whip egg whites until stiff. Gradually and gently fold egg whites into batter mixture.

6. Pour batter into a buttered and floured loaf pan. Bake for about 1 hour. The top of the cake should be firm. To test doneness, insert a toothpick into the center of the cake. When the cake is done, the toothpick should come out clean.

7. Remove from oven, cool for 10 minutes, and remove from loaf pan. Finish cooling on a wire rack. Serve in slices.*

To dress up this cake for the holidays, sift powdered sugar through a stencil to make a pretty pattern on the top of the cake.

Preparation time: 30 to 40 minutes
Cooking time: 1 hour
Makes 1 cake

Royal Mazurek / Mazurek Królewski

The traditional Easter table in a Polish home is laden with a variety of wonderful desserts.

1 c. (2 sticks) butter or margarine, softened

1¼ c. sugar

1 c. finely ground almonds

1 tsp. vanilla extract

grated rind of 1 orange*, or about 2 tbsp. dried grated orange peel

5 egg whites

1½ c. all-purpose flour

Icing:

1 c. powdered sugar

2 tsp. lemon juice

1. Preheat oven to 350°F.

2. Grease and flour a medium cookie sheet.

3. In a large mixing bowl, combine butter and sugar and beat at high speed for 5 minutes. Add almonds, vanilla extract, and orange rind and mix well.

4. In a medium mixing bowl, beat egg whites until stiff. Gradually fold flour then egg whites into butter and sugar mixture and mix gently.

5. Spread over cookie sheet and bake for 40 minutes, or until golden brown.

6. While mazurek is cooling, prepare icing by combining powdered sugar and lemon juice. When mazurek is cool, spread icing over top. Cut into small squares and serve.

Use a potato peeler or a zester to gently remove peel in small strips from the orange. Try to avoid getting the white pith, which has a bitter taste. Chop or mince the peel with a knife for even smaller pieces.

Preparation time: 20 to 30 minutes
Baking time: 40 minutes
Makes about 40 squares

Orange and lemon give this simple mazurek a springtime flavor.

Index

About the Author

Danuta Zamojska-Hutchins was born and raised in Warsaw, Poland. Before coming to the United States, she studied English literature at Warsaw University. She still has strong ties with Poland and visits her homeland frequently to attend family reunions and scholarly conferences and to do research at the many universities there. Zamojska-Hutchins has always enjoyed cooking, and she often makes Polish feasts for her family and friends. Her other interests include painting, making porcelain pottery, cross-country skiing, hiking, and swimming.

Photo Acknowledgments The photographs in this book are reproduced courtesy of: © Steve Raymer/CORBIS, pp. 2–3; © Walter and Louiseann Pietrowicz/September 8th Stock, pp. 4 (left), 5 (left and right), 18, 30, 41, 49, 50, 53, 59, 60, 65, 66, 69; © Robert L. and Diane Wolfe, pp. 4 (right), 6, 36, 45, 46; © János Kalmár, pp. 10, 16, 26; © Trip/A Gasson, p. 13; © Trip/Z Harasym, p. 15.

Cover photos: © Robert L. and Diane Wolfe (top front); © Walter and Louiseann Pietrowicz/September 8th Stock (bottom front, back, spine).

The illustrations on pp. 7, 19, 27, 31, 32, 33, 35, 37, 38, 39, 40, 44, 47, 48, 51, 52, 55, 56, 61, 62, 63, 64, 67, 68 and the map on page 8 are by Tim Seeley.